The Stock Market Crash of 1929

Scott Ingram

WORLD ALMANAC® LIBRARY

Please visit our web site at: **www.worldalmanaclibrary.com**
For a free color catalog describing World Almanac® Library's list of high-quality
books and multimedia programs, call 1-800-848-2928 (USA) or 1-800-387-3178
(Canada). World Almanac® Library's fax: (414) 332-3567.

Library of Congress Cataloging-in-Publication Data

Ingram, Scott (William Scott).
    The stock market crash of 1929 / by Scott Ingram.
        p. cm. — (Landmark events in American history)
    Includes bibliographical references and index.
    ISBN 0-8368-5397-0 (lib. bdg.)
    ISBN 0-8368-5425-X (softcover)
    1. Depressions—1929—United States—Juvenile literature.   2. New York Stock
Exchange—Juvenile literature.   3. United States—Economic conditions—1918-
1945—Juvenile literature.   4. Stock Market Crash, 1929—Juvenile literature.
I. Title. II. Series.
    HB37171929.I48   2004
    338.5'42'097309043—dc22   2004042000

First published in 2005 by
World Almanac® Library
330 West Olive Street, Suite 100
Milwaukee, WI 53212 USA

Copyright © 2005 by World Almanac® Library.

Produced by Discovery Books
Editor: Sabrina Crewe
Designer and page production: Sabine Beaupré
Photo researcher: Sabrina Crewe
Maps and diagrams: Stefan Chabluk
World Almanac® Library editorial direction: Mark J. Sachner
World Almanac® Library editor: Jenette Donovan Guntly
World Almanac® Library art direction: Tammy West
World Almanac® Library production: Jessica Morris

Photo credits: Corbis: cover, pp. 4, 5, 6, 7, 8 (both), 10, 11, 12, 13, 14, 15, 16, 17,
18, 19, 20, 21, 22, 23, 25, 26, 28, 29, 30, 33, 34, 35, 36, 37, 38, 39, 40, 41, 42, 43.

Printed in Canada

1 2 3 4 5 6 7 8 9 08 07 06 05 04

Contents

Introduction

Wall Street

In the 1600s, Dutch settlers built a wall on the southern tip of Manhattan Island to ward off attacks by other groups. Three centuries later, New York City had grown up. On the site of the long-forgotten wall was Wall Street, a busy hub of the financial world. Buildings on Wall Street included several of the world's largest investment banks, the Sub Treasury (a holding location for government funds), and the New York Stock Exchange. Wall Street is still the center of American business today.

A view of Wall Street in the early 1900s. The Sub Treasury building is on the right.

A Busy Day

Thursday, October 24, 1929, was a busy day at the New York **Stock** Exchange on Wall Street in Manhattan. The exchange was the main financial center for American investors. For most of the 1920s, people with money to **invest** had been eagerly buying **shares** in large companies. If the companies made **profits**, the value of the investors' shares rose.

Panic

By October 24, 1929, however, the value of most stocks had been sinking for more than six weeks. That morning, the value of shares on the New York Stock Exchange dropped severely as soon as the market opened. As the news spread, investors rushed to sell their shares and cut their losses. The huge rush to sell only caused the stock market to drop faster.

In order to prevent a massive financial loss, New York's most powerful bankers and brokers agreed to invest $30 million of their own money in the stock market to prevent it from collapsing altogether. At first, the strategy worked. On Friday and Saturday, share prices remained steady. On Monday, however, the value of stocks fell again. This time, bankers had no more money to support the falling share prices. The stock market collapsed on what is now known as "Black Tuesday," October 29, 1929.

The Crash and the Great Depression

The six-day period from October 24 to October 29, 1929, is known today as the stock market crash. It marked the beginning of one of the darkest periods in American history. By early 1930, businesses and banks across the country had failed. By 1932, one of every four American workers was jobless. The Great **Depression** gripped the nation.

The stock market crash had a huge impact on all industries. Even *Variety*, the entertainment newspaper, covered the story.

The Story on the Tape
"But the crowds about the **ticker tapes**, like friends about the bedside of a stricken friend, reflected in their faces the story the tape was telling. There were no smiles. There were no tears either. Just the camaraderie of fellow sufferers. Everybody wanted to tell his neighbor how much he had lost. Nobody wanted to listen. It was too repetitious a tale."

The New York Times, *October 30, 1929*

The Roaring Twenties

The Decade of the Automobile

Few decades in history have had a greater influence on modern American life than the "Roaring Twenties." The most significant development of the 1920s was the widespread use of the automobile. Millions of Americans bought cars, which in turn led to the growth of modern industries such as petroleum, rubber, and steel.

More automobiles meant that better roads were needed. In the 1920s, for the first time, the **federal** government set aside funds to build interstate highways. As the roads were built, new services arose. Gas stations, garages, and roadside restaurants sprang up across the nation. Motels—a blend of the words "motor" and "hotels"—began to replace hotels.

Mass Production

One of the most important changes to the **economy** in the 1920s was the development of the assembly line in factories. The person

Henry Ford sits in his first automobile on Grand Boulevard in Detroit, Michigan, in 1896. Ford's vehicles would change the American way of life during the next thirty years.

most responsible for creating the new type of workplace was Henry Ford, a mechanic who opened a factory in 1913 to manufacture an automobile—known as the Model T Ford—that he had designed. Ford's goal was to build as many of his cars as cheaply and quickly as possible. To do this, he developed a system in which each worker did just one specific job, from welding a part of the auto frame, to tightening certain bolts, to filling the radiator with water. Workers stood in one place while a conveyor belt carried the vehicle past their positions on the assembly line.

The change in production was rapid. By 1914, an assembly line could build a Model T Ford in ninety-three minutes. By 1929, there was one car for every five Americans, or nearly 30 million automobiles.

Modern Conveniences

As the advantage of assembly lines became apparent, industries across the United States adopted them. U.S. companies quickly began turning out radios, refrigerators, washing machines, and other machines of modern life by the millions. This new method of manufacturing became known as mass production.

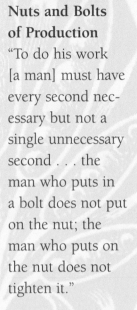

Nuts and Bolts of Production

"To do his work [a man] must have every second necessary but not a single unnecessary second . . . the man who puts in a bolt does not put on the nut; the man who puts on the nut does not tighten it."

Henry Ford, explaining the division of labor on his assembly line

Rows of mass-produced Model T cars sit in a Ford automobile plant in the 1920s. By 1925, a Model T rolled off the Ford assembly line every ten seconds.

Americans soon began buying mass-produced items in large numbers. New appliances, such as washing machines and refrigerators, became part of almost every household. These items, taken for granted today, were novelties and even luxuries at the time. They contributed to the belief among Americans in the 1920s that the nation was entering an era of great promise.

Entertainment

Mass production also brought new forms of entertainment. Americans with money to spend soon learned that radios and **phonographs** offered pleasures that were unimaginable only a decade earlier. People gathered around radio sets for their favorite shows in the same way they do with television today.

As the technology of sound recording improved, and as phonographs became

The movie industry expanded greatly during the 1920s. The poster above advertises one of Charlie Chaplin's many movies. Left, jazz trumpeter Louis Armstrong (center, in gray suit), who became famous in the nightclubs of the 1920s, is pictured with his band.

Prohibition and Gangsters

Throughout the 1920s, **Prohibition** was in force, banning the manufacture and sale of alcoholic drinks. Although it was supposed to control some of the wilder excesses of the Jazz Age, Prohibition did not work. In fact, it fuelled crime as large numbers of **bootleggers** started to make and sell liquor illegally. Nightclubs known as "speakeasies" sprang up; they sold drinks illegally to their customers and became social centers in towns and cities across the nation. Many of the most famous jazz musicians made their names in the clubs.

The bootleg operations were soon in the hands of gangs of criminals. In large cities such as New York, Chicago, and Philadelphia, rival gangs sprang up and fear ruled the streets. Owners of stores, speakeasies, and other businesses were forced to make payments to gangs or risk being killed. The most powerful gangsters, such as Al Capone of Chicago, also controlled local politicians and police officers. Violence became common as gangs fought for power. On February 14, 1929, Capone's men murdered seven people in an ambush on a rival gang, a killing called the St. Valentine's Day Massacre.

readily available, the industry of recorded music mushroomed. People began to buy records of popular music.

New kinds of music became a big part of life in the 1920s, which was also known as the "Jazz Age." Jazz, born in Southern black communities, moved into the big cities of the North. The music not only encouraged the nightclubs and dance crazes that typify the 1920s, but it also offered the first opportunity for African Americans to achieve success and wealth in white American society.

The Advertising Industry

The growth of mass production did much more than simply change the method of work; it changed the entire national economy. Because companies had increased the speed of assembling an item,

The sale of many products, including canned goods and bottled drinks, grew rapidly in the 1920s, largely because of advertising. This advertisement for grape juice is from about 1925.

they were able to produce more goods.

Businesses needed to find ways to persuade people to buy their products—if they could create a desire for their goods, more people would want to become **consumers**. Creating this desire for products led to the rapid development of a previously small industry—advertising. Prior to the 1920s, U.S. companies spent less than $1 billion per year to advertise their

What Is the Economy?

In the broadest sense, a nation's economy is its system of production, distribution, and consumption of goods and services. Beneath the overall term "economy," however, are more specific kinds of economies. The U.S. economy is a capitalist economy, which means that it is based on private ownership of **capital**—another term for money or property. (Other types of economies have government-owned businesses and property.)

For much of U.S. history, the nation's capitalist economy has been based on **free enterprise**. A free enterprise system allows private companies to produce goods and set prices without government interference. People who support free enterprise firmly believe that the government should have little control over banks and businesses.

products. By the mid-1920s, the amount spent on advertising had risen to more than $3 billion per year. Ads appeared in newspapers and magazines and on billboards and radio commercials.

Buying on Credit

While advertising created a desire for products, the cost of these products was often more than a family could afford. In order to keep up sales, companies began to sell products on **credit**. Under this arrangement, customers made a small initial payment, called a "down payment," on the cost of an item and took it home. They then promised to pay the remainder of the cost over a period of time, plus an additional sum as **interest**. This led to the key advertising phrase of the decade: "Buy now, pay later."

Selling goods to customers on credit made many companies profitable in the first half of the 1920s. In their quest to increase profits, however, companies continued to make more products. For instance, businesses made over 40 percent more goods in 1925

In the 1920s, most people did not earn enough to buy all the new and exciting products they wanted. Radios were typical of the type of appliances bought on credit.

President Calvin Coolidge believed in encouraging big business. During his presidency (1923–1929), owners of large steel, railroad, and manufacturing industries became immensely wealthy.

than they had in 1920. During that same time, however, wages increased just 8 percent. This meant that, by the middle of the decade, there were too many goods and too few customers to buy them—even on credit.

Promoting Business

Free enterprise was encouraged by the political climate of the 1920s. Calvin Coolidge, who was president from 1923 to 1929, worked to keep American business free of high **taxes** and government regulations. Yet while he claimed that the government should stay out of business, Coolidge raised tariffs—the taxes paid by foreign companies to sell their products in the United States. The higher tariffs kept foreign competitors from offering cheaper goods to American consumers, who were forced to buy only American goods.

Forgotten Farms

While government leaders focused on business, they overlooked part of the economy that had been a foundation of American life—agriculture. During World War I (1914–1918), the need for food in the United States and war-torn Europe had become critical. The federal government had paid farmers high prices for their wheat and other grains. The government had also encouraged farmers to

Changing Times
"The man who builds a factory, builds a temple. The man who works there, worships there."

Calvin Coolidge, 1926

buy more land, to use the newest farm machinery, and to produce more food. Many farmers had done so in the belief that the government support would continue.

Once the war ended, the efforts the farmers put into modernizing their methods actually hurt them. The more food they raised, the less they were paid because there was now a surplus. The federal government, which had paid farmers $2 a bushel for wheat during the war, withdrew its support, and wheat prices fell to 67¢ a bushel. At the same time, the cost of seed, farm machinery, fuel, and other necessities rose steadily.

Economic Inequality

Farmers were not the only people who were left behind in the Roaring Twenties. Beneath the explosion of production and buying were some disturbing facts. While the media portrayed the 1920s as a time when many people became wealthy overnight, almost three-fourths of American families spent their entire incomes on basic necessities such as food, clothing, and housing.

The benefits of the so-called "Coolidge Prosperity" were limited to a small percentage of the wealthiest Americans. According to studies, the wealthiest 0.1 percent of Americans in 1926 had a combined income equal to that of the bottom 42 percent of Americans. An example of this inequality was seen in the income of Henry Ford, who earned $14 million in 1927, a year when the average income of Americans was only about $1,000 a year.

Farmers in the 1920s, such as this man, were encouraged to borrow money to buy tractors and other modern equipment. They found themselves struggling with debt when the government withdrew its support for agriculture.

Chapter 2

The Booming Economy

While big business grew, it did not create wealth for the workers. These men at a General Electric plant in New York worked hard for low pay while the company made enormous profits.

Helping the Wealthy

During his time in office, President Coolidge continually used the power of the government to benefit the wealthiest Americans. One example of government assistance was the Revenue Act of 1926, which made drastic cuts in the federal income and inheritance tax rates. The main force behind the new law was Andrew Mellon, Coolidge's secretary of the treasury and one of the wealthiest people in the United States.

The Revenue Act and other tax cuts put millions of dollars into the pockets of wealthy business owners. Mellon claimed that this huge amount of money would eventually trickle down to average Americans because the business owners would reinvest the money in their own companies, enabling them to expand productivity and therefore hire more workers.

Down with Taxes

"High taxes . . . destroy individual initiative and enterprise and seriously impede the development of productive enterprise."

Andrew Mellon, 1926

Andrew Mellon (1855—1937)

Andrew W. Mellon was born in Pittsburgh, Pennsylvania, and was the son of a banker. He started a lumber business when he was seventeen, and by the age of twenty-seven, he owned his family's bank. From there, Mellon entered the oil, steel, construction, and shipbuilding industries. By 1920, he was one of the three wealthiest men in the United States. Over his lifetime, Mellon gave away huge amounts of his fortune to good causes.

Mellon served as secretary of the treasury from 1921 until 1932 under Presidents Harding, Coolidge, and Hoover. He made lowering taxes and cutting government spending his personal crusade. Congress passed six tax cuts between 1921 and 1929, and, at the same time, Mellon succeeded in greatly reducing the national debt.

In 1932, when the United States was deep in the Great Depression, Mellon left the treasury. He became the U.S. ambassador to Britain for a year before retiring from government service.

Another member of Coolidge's cabinet, secretary of commerce Herbert Hoover, also believed that the government should help big business. In his position, he allowed large corporations to buy up smaller competitors until they controlled almost all of a certain industry. U.S. Steel, for example, was allowed to buy up smaller steel companies until it had a **monopoly** on the steel market.

Bull Market

At the halfway point of Coolidge's term in 1926, most Americans believed that the United States was a land of unlimited possibilities. In the 1920s, people's view of the economy was not based on whether taxes were high or low. Instead, it was based on whether

Between 1927 and 1929, it seemed that the whole country was trying to get rich quickly and easily by investing in the stock market. Many thousands of small investors followed the price of shares, including these two visitors to the New York Stock Exchange in 1929.

the stock market was rising or falling. And, for five years—from 1924 to 1929—the value of shares on the stock market rose, a period called a "bull market."

Faith in Investments

During the rise in the stock market, no more than 2 to 4 percent of the U.S. population bought shares. When the crash happened, maybe as few as 2 million out of more than 120 million Americans actually owned shares. Nevertheless, most Americans became convinced that if the stock market increased in overall value, the entire national economy was strong.

In theory, this belief was true. In order to grow, companies needed money to hire more workers, build more factories, or produce more goods. By offering investors a chance to "share" in the growth by buying a portion of the business, companies could raise cash for their expansion. As the companies grew, the value of the investors' shares also increased.

The Stock Market

In 1792, New York businessmen and brokers met on Wall Street in lower Manhattan. There, they agreed that brokers would sell shares of stock in businesses to investors for a fee. In 1817, stockbrokers formed the New York Stock Exchange. Much of the early investment in the stock market, however, was in **bonds** sold by state governments to raise money to pay for canals and railroad lines. The first railroad stock was sold in 1830. Throughout the 1800s, railroad stock made up most of the shares traded in the market.

Hopeful Investors

Stock market investors believed that they were helping businesses strengthen the economy while making money for themselves at the same time. Investors were eager to buy any stock. During a bull market, investors expected every stock to rise, regardless of whether the company was financially healthy.

Many companies, therefore, whether financially sound or not, brought in enormous amounts of money from the sale of shares. This money was invested in building new factories, buying new machines, and hiring more workers. This, in turn, led to greater production of goods.

American industry was eventually producing far more goods than could be sold. Many companies nevertheless continued to offer shares to eager investors, who willingly bought them in the belief that they would continue to increase in value. At the time, there were no federal regulations that controlled the number of shares a company could offer, so business owners were free to sell more shares than their companies were actually worth.

There were more than twenty U.S. stock exchanges in 1929, but the New York Stock Exchange (seen below, decorated for the holidays) was the oldest and biggest. It remains the principal U.S. financial exchange today.

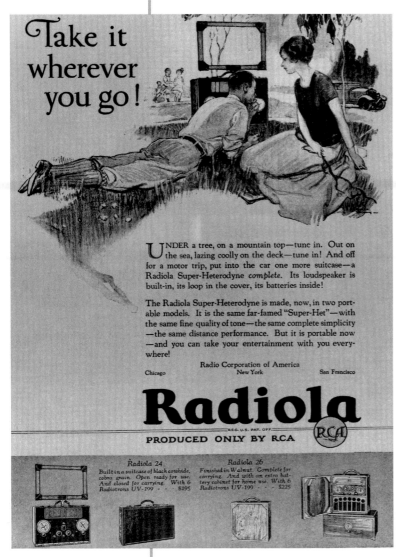

In the 1920s, people borrowed money to buy shares on margin in companies that were growing rapidly, such as RCA. When RCA stock shot up, investors felt they were rich, even if they were actually in debt from having borrowed money to buy the shares.

Buying on Margin

Many people who invested in the stock market did not have enough money to buy shares of stock. Determined not to miss out on the easy money offered by the stock market, they paid what they could and borrowed the remaining money from brokers (who borrowed it from banks), a practice called "buying on margin."

Buying on margin worked in much the same way as buying on credit. In early 1928, for example, a share of stock in the Radio Corporation of America (RCA) sold for $85. An investor who wanted to buy a share of RCA stock could put $10 of his or her own money down and borrow the remaining $75 from a stockbroker, who would then charge a 5 percent fee of $3.75.

By the end of 1928, the value of RCA stock had risen to $420 a share. Once an investor repaid the $75 he or she had borrowed, plus the fee, the original $10 investment was worth $341.25.

Buying on margin worked well as long as stocks continued to rise. If a stock lost value, however, a broker issued a "margin call." This meant that the investor had to repay all of the money—loan and fee—immediately or face legal charges. Few investors considered this possibility in 1928, and buying on margin became the chief means of paying for shares among American investors.

A New President

In 1928, Herbert Hoover was elected president, to succeed Coolidge in 1929. On New Year's Day in 1929, an editorial in the *New York Times,* one of the most respected newspapers in the nation, declared, "It has been twelve months of . . . wonderful prosperity. If there is any way of judging the future by the past, this new year will be one of felicitation and hopefulness." Herbert Hoover took office on March 4, 1929, and gave an inaugural address filled with optimism.

Bright Future

"Ours is a land rich in resources . . . filled with millions of happy homes, blessed with comfort and opportunity. In no nation are the institutions of progress more advanced. . . . I have no fears for the future. . . . It is bright with hope."

Herbert Hoover, inaugural address, March 1929

Herbert Hoover is inaugurated as president in March 1929.

Signs of Trouble

The Federal Reserve Board

Even as Hoover was assuring Americans of their happy future, the Federal **Reserve** Board was meeting behind closed doors. The board was a group of presidential appointees that kept an eye on the nation's banks.

The Federal Reserve

In 1929, the stock market crash caused a run on this bank in New Jersey. Most of the bank's customers went to withdraw their money at one time.

Before the days of the Federal Reserve, if a large number of people decided to withdraw their savings from a particular bank at the same time—an event that is called a "run"—a panic developed because the banks kept only small amounts of cash on hand. After a widespread run and panic in 1907, politicians began to call for a system of reserve banks under federal control. In 1913, a new law divided the nation into several banking regions, with a central Federal Reserve bank in each. The Federal Reserve banks held cash reserves and loaned money to member banks in each of their regions. The law also created the Federal Reserve Board of Governors, a commission appointed by the president to oversee the banks.

Board members were alarmed by the enormous amounts of money that had been loaned to stockbrokers by banks. The brokers in turn had loaned that money to investors, who used it to buy stocks on margin. Reserve Board members feared that any decrease in stock value would prevent investors from repaying brokers. That would mean that brokers could not repay the banks, which would put the nation's banking system at risk.

Lenders at Risk

By 1929, brokers had loaned over $8 billion to investors for buying on margin. Also by that time, there were so many eager investors that some companies began to invest their increasingly large profits with stockbrokers. Instead of expanding their businesses, companies acted like banks by loaning cash to brokers, who then loaned it to investors buying on margin. So it wasn't just the banks that would suffer if brokers were unable to pay back the money, but businesses, too. It was a precarious situation, and the Federal Reserve Board was worried.

Raising Interest Rates

The board decided to raise **interest rates** for loans between banks with the expectation that their action would cause other lending rates to rise. This rise, they hoped, would reduce the amount of money people could afford to borrow, and thus slow the cycle of borrowing and buying. The action by the Federal Reserve caused a one-day stock market crash on March 25, 1929, when decreasing sales caused the entire market to lose value. The market recovered, but the brief fall foreshadowed ominous events to come.

Clerks in a brokers' office near Wall Street read the latest prices on a ticker tape. By October 1929, when this photograph was taken, frantic buying and selling meant stock prices changed minute to minute.

Ignoring the Problems

The stock market continued to rise throughout the summer of 1929. American investors continued to buy stocks with little or no understanding of their value.

It was not only average investors who did not understand the growing threat of the expanding stock market. Economists and financial experts had also become convinced that the true measure of an economy's health was the stock market. They began to overlook traditional measures of economic health, such as house construction, sales of goods, workers'

Charles Merrill (1885—1956)

Charles Merrill began his working career as an investment banker before World War I. He made a fortune and founded one of the United States' first wire houses, or brokerage firms with branch offices in large cities across the country. By February 1929, Merrill was so certain that the stock market was headed for collapse that he sold all of his stock and advised his clients to pull their money out of the market. Widely criticized for his decision in February, Merrill became a celebrity when his prediction came true in October. He later founded the investment company Merrill Lynch, which brought stock market investing to a wide range of Americans.

wages, or the financial health of banks. By any of these measures, the economy was actually beginning to slow down. For instance, between 1923 and 1929, while workers increased production of goods by 32 percent, average wages increased by only 8 percent. Yet stocks continued to rise in value.

By September 1929, about 40 percent of stocks on the market had values based on little more than "expert" opinion. Prices rose simply because investors had faith that the entire stock market would go up. Those who blindly bought stock were ignoring basic weaknesses in the national economy.

Early Warnings

In 1928, banker Charles Merrill had become uneasy about the state of the stock market and overall economy. Merrill had appealed to President Coolidge to speak out against **speculating**, which was pushing the market to dangerous heights. Coolidge had ignored Merrill's pleas, saying that the enormous amount of money invested in the stock market was due to "the natural expansion of business."

Charles Merrill, who foresaw the looming stock market crisis, was good at spotting trends ahead of other people. He was among the first to realize that chain stores would lead the future retail market, and his bank financed early chains, including Safeway Stores, shown here.

Chapter 4

The Crash

The chart on the right shows how stock prices of five major U.S. companies, at their peak in early September, began a downward slide in October 1929.

Bear Market

On September 3, 1929, the imbalance in the overall economy reached the stock market. After that date, stocks began to lose value as companies reported declining sales and smaller-than-expected profits. Unlike the one-day fall of the market six months before, this downward movement continued. Stock experts called this a "bear market," the name for an extended period of falling stock values.

By the third week of October 1929, stock prices had fallen steadily—but not drastically—for six weeks. Then, on Monday, October 21, prices suddenly dropped across the market. On Tuesday and Wednesday, October 22 and 23, the market remained steady, neither rising nor falling.

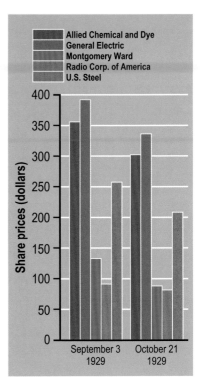

Black Thursday

At the opening bell on Thursday, October 24, the New York Stock Exchange became a beehive of activity. Many people, becoming fearful of falling prices, began selling their shares. Brokers pushed and shoved around trading desks where the action was heaviest. This was where the giants of the market, such as General Electric and U.S. Steel, were traded.

Fear spread across the floor because once an order to sell shares was placed, a broker had to move quickly to fill the order. Stocks don't sell for fixed prices—a stock market is like an auction, where buyers seek sellers and vice versa. Prices can change all the time. And that was how the morning of "Black Thursday" unfolded.

A few hands were raised as bidding for stocks began, but the ticker machines that communicated prices began to fall behind on

The New York Stock Exchange

In 1865, the New York Stock Exchange (NYSE) opened its first permanent building near Wall Street in New York City. By 1867, the tickers were sending stock prices across the country. From 1878, the telephone enabled investors to call in orders to brokers at the stock exchange.

In 1903, the NYSE moved to the building on Wall Street that it occupies today. Inside the NYSE was the trading floor, more than 36,000 square feet (3,350 square meters) in area, where most of the daily activity took place. In some ways, the trading floor resembled a huge train terminal. Instead of one main ticket or information booth, however, there were more than five hundred horseshoe-shaped trading desks. Each company that offered stock had a trading desk staffed by uniformed clerks who handled paperwork, like ticket agents in a train station.

The New York Stock Exchange trading floor hummed with activity in the 1920s.

Every day, trading opened and closed at the sound of a loud bell ringing. On the crowded floor, brokers, representing large and small investors, shouted orders and gathered around tickers. Through the crowds and confusion, messengers and ticker tape boys dashed around, carrying orders and stock updates.

Mounted police officers control the crowds hanging around on Wall Street in October 1929. People gathered hoping to learn the latest news of the stock market.

current prices. As word of another sudden loss spread, investors scrambled to communicate with their brokers and tell them to sell. Worried investors tried to call brokers at the stock exchange itself, but the telephone lines were busy.

Investors across the country, unable to learn the latest price changes, began to panic and place sell orders without even knowing the current prices. The huge number of sell orders coming into the stock exchange caused the prices of stocks to fall ever more rapidly. The rapidly changing prices caused tickers to fall more than an hour behind in sending out updates.

Technical Condition
"There has been a little distress selling on the Stock Exchange . . . due to a technical condition of the market."

Thomas Lamont of Morgan Investments, addressing reporters, Thursday, October 24, 1929

The Panic Begins
People gathered outside the exchanges and brokerages, and police were dispatched to ensure peace. By late morning, crowds of

The Dow Jones Index

The Dow Jones Industrial Average was created in 1896 to be a guide to the overall activity of the stock market and the price of shares. When the Dow Jones index is high, the market is doing well. A change in the Dow Jones figure from one day to the next shows that the average price of shares on the index has risen or fallen. In 1929, the Dow Jones based its daily figure on the price of stock in thirty leading U.S. companies, such as U.S. Steel and the Radio Corporation of America. This chart shows what happened to the value of those companies before, during, and after the stock market crash of 1929, as reflected by the Dow Jones index.

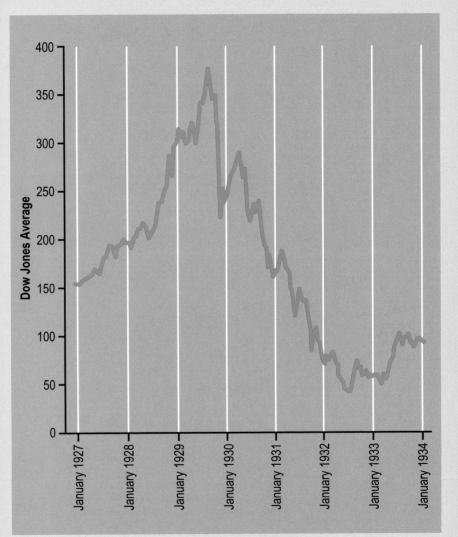

investors were trying to force their way inside the New York Stock Exchange to contact their brokers. Police came in to control rioting by some of the wealthiest people in American business.

Pooling Resources

At lunchtime on October 24, 1929, the wealthiest bankers and brokers in New York City gathered to address the crisis. The only way to avoid a massive stock market collapse, they agreed, was to pool their funds and buy shares. By early afternoon, more than $30 million in personal funds was in the hands of the vice president of the New York Stock Exchange, Richard Whitney.

At 1:00 P.M., Whitney walked onto the trading floor. The crowd hushed as he asked for the latest bid on U.S. Steel. Someone in the crowd shouted, "$195." Whitney promptly announced that he was buying ten thousand shares of U.S. Steel at $205. He then sent errand boys off to brokers with orders for thousands of shares of large-company stocks at far above their current price. By the end of the day that came to be known as "Black Thursday," the losses of the morning had been stopped.

On Thursday, October 24—the first day of the crash—it was the small investors who were hit most by the drop in prices. On that day, this group waited nervously outside the exchange for news of their investments.

A Small Improvement

If not for the $30 million, the losses of Black Thursday would have been much worse. The value of department store Montgomery Ward's stock, for example, had been $83 a share that morning but had dropped to $50 by noon. Whitney's efforts had allowed the stock to end the day at $74 a share. Nevertheless, the fall on Thursday basically wiped out the small investors—those who owned fewer than five thousand shares of stock.

By Friday, the previous day's price drop was considered by large investors to be little more than a "correction," or a fall to balance the previous huge rises. Stocks rose slightly then and also during the half-day trading session on Saturday. Over the weekend, clerks and errand boys worked around the clock to log transactions. Messengers carried the latest information to brokerage houses and

Clerks on Wall Street worked long hours without sleep, trying to keep up with changing prices and their customers' orders.

Nothing Left

"The first day of October in 1929 made me feel like I was rich [but after the crash] I was wiped out. . . . I had nothing left."

George Mehales, a Greek immigrant who lost his business and all his money because of the 1929 stock market crash

Suddenly, people who thought they were rich had nothing. This investor, wiped out by his losses, tried to raise cash by selling his luxury car at a bargain price.

banks on Wall Street. Some stock exchange workers worked forty hours straight, sleeping on cots set up on the trading floor so they would not have to go home.

President Hoover addressed the nation on October 25, 1929. He tried to reassure Americans, saying, "The fundamental business of the country, that is production of commodities, is on a sound and prosperous basis." Yet even as Hoover spoke, nervous brokers were sending out margin calls that had been delayed by the chaos on Thursday. Investors continued to place sell orders to prevent further losses and to raise funds to pay the margin calls.

The Small Investors

By 1929, because of the opportunities offered by buying on margin—and of course, pure greed—many people had invested in the stock market who could not afford the risk. Individual investors, although they lost smaller amounts, were hit hard by the margin calls. People not only sold their stock, but they sold cars, jewelry, even their homes, to try to meet their debts to brokers. If the money was not there when the broker demanded it, the stock would be sold, and the investor would have nothing left except his loan debt to the broker.

Black Monday

When the opening bell rang on Monday, October 28, there was a mood of optimism on the trading floor. Many of the remaining investors believed that even if the market began to fall, bankers would again step forward as they had on Thursday.

An hour after the opening bell, however, it became apparent that the market was headed down once again. There was almost no business because the losses of the previous week had ended any further investment by the general public. Those who still had profits in the market saw them slipping away. Those who had losses feared they might worsen still further. Panic selling broke out again. Suddenly, investors who could not buy enough shares several months earlier could not sell their shares fast enough. Bankers and brokers were helpless to stop the fall. On Black Monday, the market lost more than 12 percent of its value, far worse than on the previous Thursday.

Black Tuesday

The crash of Black Monday largely ruined wealthy people, large banks, and giant investment houses. The next day, October 29, was one of the worst days in the history of the New York Stock Exchange. At the opening bell, the trading floor was eerily quiet.

Within a few hours, prices fell so low that all of the financial gains of the previous year were lost. On Black Tuesday alone, shares of the sixteen largest companies on the stock exchange lost almost $3 billion, a sum the size of the entire federal budget for 1929. Millions of investors and brokers were completely wiped out. The stock market had collapsed.

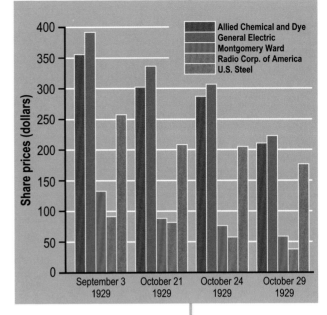

Vanished Hopes

"Wall Street was a street of vanished hopes, of curiously silent apprehension and of a sort of paralyzed hypnosis yesterday. Men and women crowded the brokerage offices, even those who have been long since wiped out, and followed the figures on the tape."

The New York Times, *October 30, 1929*

In the course of a few days in October, the share prices of some of the largest and most profitable U.S. companies fell drastically. Worse was yet to come.

Chapter 5

The Great Depression

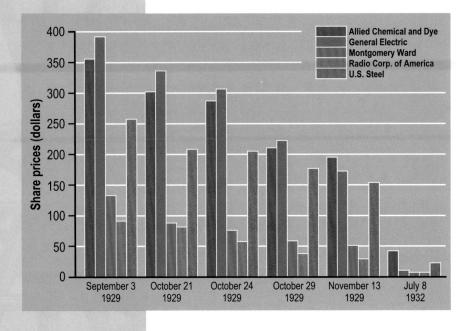

Allied Chemical and Dye
General Electric
Montgomery Ward
Radio Corp. of America
U.S. Steel

By July 1932, with the United States in the grip of the Great Depression, share prices hit their lowest point. Even the prices at the time of the crash looked pretty good in comparison.

Causes of the Great Depression

Many people think that the 1929 stock market crash caused the Great Depression that followed. The U.S. economy, however, was already in deep trouble, a fact that had been disguised by soaring stock prices and the high spending of the wealthy. In 1929, most people in the United States were poor, the demand for consumer items and housing was slowing down, and the nation's many independent banks were not very stable. In addition, the United States was owed billions of dollars by countries in Europe that couldn't afford to pay the debt.

The stock market collapse did, however, contribute greatly to the difficult years to follow. Some effects were immediate. Business owners watched the worth of their companies vanish overnight. Stockbrokers were ruined when investors could not meet their margin calls. Many investors lost everything they had. Above all, the crash caused people to lose confidence in the economy.

The Economy in Ruins

Other consequences soon followed. Large and small manufacturing companies began to lay off workers and close factories when demand for their goods dropped. The massive loss of jobs caused millions of people to default, or miss payments, on goods they had bought on credit, causing more economic problems.

Banks, too, fell under the rapidly worsening economy. Those that had loaned money to brokers found themselves short of funds.

At the same time, people began a run on the banks to withdraw their savings. The number of withdrawal requests grew too quickly for even the Federal Reserve, and banks across the nation began to close their doors. In the last four months of 1929, more than six hundred banks failed. By the end of 1930, more than four thousand had shut down. People who had saved for years to buy a home or educate their children had their dreams shattered when they lost their savings. Older Americans who planned to use their savings for retirement suddenly found themselves penniless.

President Hoover's Response

In November 1929, President Hoover persuaded Congress to cut income taxes in the hope that people would start spending again and revive the economy. Most families, however, didn't pay much tax anyway after all the previous tax cuts, and the new cut made little difference—a family earning $2,000 a year had its income tax reduced from $2.80 to $1.00. The wealthy received much more benefit, but they were unwilling to spend because they had no confidence in the economy.

The United States was hit hard and fast by unemployment when failed businesses closed their doors. These unemployed men were lined up outside a soup kitchen in Chicago that handed out free food.

Hoovervilles

As people lost their jobs, they also lost their homes. Thousands of Americans who had once had houses, employment, and hope for the future were forced to seek shelter in **shantytowns**. These towns for the homeless became known as "Hoovervilles" after the increasingly unpopular president. The clusters of huts appeared on vacant lots in cities and suburbs. They were built of scrap metal, wood, cardboard, or anything else that could be found in dumps. Hoovervilles were without plumbing, electricity, or water supply. The people who lived in them had no money to buy medicine or even food, and many became sick and malnourished.

A Hooverville in Seattle, Washington.

By 1930, Hoover was well aware of the financial ruin that faced the nation, but he did not want to alarm Americans by calling the economic collapse a panic. Instead, he used the term by which the era would become known—"depression." As people began to suffer from unemployment, Hoover asked cities, states, and private charities to feed the hungry. True to his political principles, Hoover refused to offer federal **welfare** or unemployment assistance to Americans in need.

Rural Devastation

The Great Depression hit everyone, but it was worst for rural Americans. By 1929, low crop prices wiped out any profits, and farmers could not meet their loan payments to banks. This caused a collapse of the rural banking system.

Then, just when it seemed things could not get worse, one of the worst droughts in history hit the nation in the 1930s. On farms from Tennessee to Oklahoma, in an area that became known as the Dust Bowl, crops failed and livestock died. In rural areas, desperate farmers rebelled. Several hundred farmers broke into food stores in Oklahoma. In Iowa and Nebraska, farmers who could no longer pay their bank loans used pitchforks and axes to drive off police who came to repossess their homes and belongings.

Homeless and Hungry

During President Hoover's term in office, the average weekly wages of workers had fallen from $25 to $17. Those who earned money, however, were considered fortunate. Millions of American workers —about one in every four—were unemployed. Between 1930 and 1932, a million families lost their farms.

The numbers of the homeless and hungry kept growing. Local charities fed thousands of people who stood in line for hours to get

During the Dust Bowl years, farming families simply abandoned their homes and fields to the dust and left to try and make a living elsewhere.

The Bonus Army

Unemployed veterans of World War I camp outside the Capitol in July 1932.

One of the low points of the Depression occurred in 1932, when thousands of jobless military veterans formed the Bonus Army. They marched to Washington, D.C., to demand that the benefits promised to them when they enlisted to fight in World War I be paid by the government. Thousands of desperate men camped in Washington, demanding government help. Instead of giving aid, Hoover called out the U.S. Army to drive the veterans out of town. The event triggered nationwide outrage. "What a pitiful spectacle," declared a newspaper article. "If the Army must be called out to make war on unarmed citizens, this is no longer America."

a free meal. About two of every three children in New York City suffered from malnutrition.

The Election of 1932

By 1932, the U.S. faced the worst economic crisis in its history. In the presidential contest that year, the Republican Party nominated Hoover to run for a second term. Democrats nominated Franklin D. Roosevelt, the governor of New York. During his campaign, Roosevelt blamed Republican policies for the stock market collapse. He promised Americans the New Deal, a group of federal programs to help farmers and workers. Hoover, meanwhile, blamed the stock market collapse on events beyond government control and claimed that Roosevelt's ideas would destroy the American way of life.

In November 1932, American voters totally rejected the ideas of people like Coolidge, Hoover, and Mellon, who

A homeless family walks along a highway in Oklahoma in 1938. Many families became migrant workers (workers who moved from place to place) during the Great Depression. They went wherever there was hope of finding temporary work.

held that the government should not intrude in business or assist those ruined by the crash. Many Americans had lost all trust in business and elected leaders. They had basic doubts about the U.S. economic system and about the very nature of government itself.

Roosevelt Takes Over

Roosevelt was elected by a wide margin, and the Democratic Party won control of Congress. Roosevelt's first action after taking office in March 1933 was to declare a national bank holiday and close all banks. He declared that only banks whose records passed federal inspection would be allowed to reopen. Most banks were closed for less than ten days. By mid-summer, more than three-fourths of the banks in the nation were open again. The effect of the closures was that the American people once again felt safe depositing their

Vigorous Action

"We do not distrust the future of democracy . . . the people of the United States . . . want direct, vigorous action."

Franklin D. Roosevelt, inaugural address, March 1933

A 1938 cartoon depicts President Roosevelt in the middle of a group of children symbolizing New Deal programs. The various employment projects restored morale even though times remained tough for several more years.

money in banks. This confidence grew when laws were passed that insured people's deposits of up to $5,000 with government funds.

Regulating the Market

In 1934, President Roosevelt created the Securities and Exchange Commission (SEC) to oversee the stock market. The SEC was given the power to examine stocks offered for sale to determine whether companies were truthful about their financial status. In addition, the SEC was given the power to regulate the activities of brokers and to prosecute brokers who engaged in fraud.

At the same time, Roosevelt gave the Federal Reserve Board the power to set controls on buying on margin in the market. The risky practice was made less dangerous by this government control.

Work for the People

Roosevelt also convinced Congress to create federal agencies that would assist Americans. The first agency, created in 1933, was the Civilian Conservation Corps (CCC), which provided jobs for unemployed men and women in rural areas. CCC workers planted trees, stocked rivers with fish, and cleared wilderness trails in national parks and forests. They also restored famous battle sites from the American Revolution and Civil War.

After the CCC, Roosevelt and Congress created the Public Works Administration (PWA). The PWA hired unemployed workers to build schools, hospitals, and public housing projects. In 1933, the Civil Works Administration (CWA) was created. It employed more than 4 million Americans in smaller-scale public works projects such as improving parks, playgrounds, and roads.

In 1935, most of the employment programs were combined under the Works Progress Administration (WPA). This enormous government operation hired workers to build highways, dams, bridges, and many public buildings in Washington, D.C. In addition, the WPA employed writers, artists, actors, and musicians. They wrote guidebooks, painted murals on government buildings, and gave public performances.

Clash of Beliefs

Despite government efforts, the nation remained trapped in the Great Depression throughout Roosevelt's first term. Nevertheless, many lower-class and middle-class Americans were encouraged that the federal government was taking steps to solve the problem.

Thousands of WPA employees worked on highways and city streets. These men were widening a road to accommodate automobile traffic.

Roosevelt was the first president to speak directly to the American people over the radio. His broadcasts, called "Fireside Chats," helped Americans feel more connected to government than ever before.

Others, especially wealthy businesspeople and those who followed the beliefs of Coolidge and Hoover, complained that the government had become too **radical**. These people, generally called conservatives, claimed that Roosevelt had made the federal government too powerful. The American public, however, solidly supported Roosevelt, and he was reelected by a wide margin in 1936.

Franklin Delano Roosevelt (1882—1945)

Franklin Delano Roosevelt, a distant cousin of President Theodore Roosevelt, came from a wealthy New York family. After training as a lawyer, Roosevelt entered politics at a young age—he became a state senator in New York before the age of thirty. In the summer of 1921, Roosevelt was stricken with polio, eventually becoming unable to walk. His determination to overcome his disability won wide admiration. In 1928, Roosevelt was elected governor of New York, and he was reelected in 1932, the year he also ran for president. His huge popularity as governor and president was well-founded: Roosevelt was a strong leader determined to help Americans through the Great Depression. He went on to lead the nation through its next great crisis when the United States entered World War II in 1941. Roosevelt was the only president ever elected to four terms. He died in 1945, soon after beginning his fourth term.

During his second term, Roosevelt put in place many government programs that are taken for granted in modern American life. These included unemployment insurance and Social Security. In 1940, Roosevelt broke the presidential tradition of serving only two terms and ran successfully for a third term.

Roosevelt's Legacy

The president strongly believed that his new policies would bring the nation out of the Great Depression. In truth, the decade that followed the collapse of the stock market was a complete reversal of the prosperous decade that had preceded it, and it was not until World War II began that a real recovery took hold. What Roosevelt did achieve, however, was some financial regulation and stability. The Roosevelt administration, while it did not immediately solve the grim economic problems, did take steps to assert federal control over business to protect Americans. As a result, faith in government and in the economy slowly returned.

The Roosevelt years also brought fundamental changes to the relationship between the government and the people. The support that the average citizen receives from the government today, whether from unemployment insurance, Social Security, or other government programs, was created during those dark days in American history.

Posters such as this one were displayed in post offices throughout the country to introduce people to the new programs of the Roosevelt years. For the first time, the government offered pensions for retired people and welfare programs for the unemployed.

Conclusion

The Impact of the Crash

Apart from the Civil War and the major wars of the twentieth century, few other events changed life in the United States more than the stock market crash of 1929. Although only a small percentage of the population actually invested money in stocks, most Americans had an unshakeable belief that the stock market represented all that was "right" about the American economy.

Along with faith in the stock market, the belief that business should be free of government oversight was a core value of the 1920s. At a time when common sense could have prevented economic disaster, however, no one in government or business would take responsibility for speaking the truth to Americans. As a result, virtually worthless stocks were sold to unsuspecting investors who gambled enormous sums. The stock market collapse over five days in October caused greater damage to the United States than just the loss of personal fortunes. It created doubt and mistrust in banks, businesses, and brokers—the foundation of the financial world.

The trading floor of the New York Stock Exchange is just as busy today as it was in the 1920s. Instead of ticker tapes, there are now computer screens and cellular phones.

The Stock Market Today

The New York Stock Exchange building is housed in the same building as it was in October 1929. With new technology, investors from around the world can complete transactions with brokers almost instantaneously. The U.S. economy has become much more intertwined with the global economy, and many factors now govern what happens to the price of shares at the NYSE. One thing, however, is constant: As in 1929, stock investment is a risk.

The stock market crash changed the relationship between investors and their money. Although some investors have gained sudden wealth in the stock market in recent years, there are fewer reports of overnight millionaires than there were in the 1920s. On the other hand, more Americans are investing in the stock market now than ever before.

Today, many small investors follow the ups and downs of the stock market. The NASDAQ, an index similar to the Dow Jones, displays share prices and other financial news to the public on its giant screen in Times Square, New York City.

The Legacy of the Stock Market Crash of 1929

Because of the 1929 crash, certain safeguards were introduced into the U.S. financial world. Prices of shares may rise and fall, but the American economy —and the stock market itself—is protected against collapse. The Securities and Exchange Commission gives the federal government the power to prevent the type of abuses that caused the crash in 1929. The additional power of the Federal Reserve to prevent excessive buying on margin has also helped the government protect investors from unscrupulous brokers. While events such as a severe, one-day crash in 1987 caused losses for some investors, for example, there was no panic as there was in 1929 because people had faith in the stock market—and the government.

Time Line

1817	▪	New York Stock Exchange is founded.
1896	▪	Dow Jones Industrial Average is created.
1903	▪	New York Stock Exchange moves to current home on Wall Street.
1913	▪	Federal Reserve Bank system is created.
		Henry Ford opens automobile manufacturing factory.
1920	▪	Prohibition begins.
1923	▪	Vice President Calvin Coolidge becomes president after the death of President Warren Harding.
1924	▪	Coolidge is elected president.
1926	▪	Revenue Act is enacted by Congress.
1929	▪	March 4: Herbert Hoover is inaugurated as president.
		March 25: Federal Reserve Board raises interest rates, causing one-day stock market crash on March 25.
		September 3: Stocks begin to decline.
		October 21: Stock prices drop suddenly.
		October 24: Black Thursday.
		October 28: Black Monday.
		October 29: Black Tuesday.
		November: Government cuts income taxes in an unsuccessful attempt to revive the economy.
		Great Depression begins.
1930	▪	Bank panic spreads across United States.
		Beginning of Dust Bowl conditions in the Midwest.
1932	▪	Bonus Army marches to Washington, D.C.
		Franklin D. Roosevelt is elected president.
1933	▪	March: President Roosevelt declares national bank holiday for federal bank inspections.
		New Deal programs restructure the banking system and initiate government-sponsored projects to employ millions.
1934	▪	Securities and Exchange Commission is created.
1936	▪	Roosevelt is elected to second term.
1939	▪	World War II begins.
1940	▪	Roosevelt is elected to third term.
1941	▪	United States enters World War II.
		Great Depression ends.

Glossary

bond: certificate issued by a government that promises to pay or pay back a certain amount of money by a certain date.

bootlegger: person who makes or sells illegal liquor.

capital: wealth or assets, such as land, that can be used to create more wealth.

consumer: person who buys and uses goods.

credit: amount allowed or loaned to a person for future repayment.

depression: long period of time when the economy slows down, jobs are lost, and people stop spending.

economy: system of producing and distributing goods and services.

federal: having to do with national government.

free enterprise: business activity that is not subject to control and regulation.

interest: amount of extra money paid back on a borrowed sum of money.

interest rates: percentage of interest charged on loans or paid on savings. Interest rates given and charged by banks go up and down according to the rate set by the U.S. government.

invest: put money into something in the hope of making more money.

monopoly: total control of a particular industry or market.

phonograph: early music player.

profit: gain made by a business or person after all expenses are paid.

Prohibition: period from 1920 to 1933 when the sale and manufacture of liquor was banned throughout the United States. (To prohibit something means to stop it happening.)

radical: very different or extreme.

reserve: amount kept aside or held back for a special reason, such as a sudden shortage or emergency.

shantytown: group of roughly built shelters or houses.

share: one of a number of equal parts of equal value into which a company's stock is divided. The price of the share goes up and down according to the wealth and success of the company.

speculate: invest in risky business schemes in the hope of making a profit.

stock: value of a company that can be owned by one owner or sold in shares to investors who want to buy a part of the company and benefit from its profits.

tax: sum charged by the government on purchases or income and used to pay for services or costs of governing.

ticker tape: paper tape that prints out information sent to tickers, which are machines that can receive information (such as share prices) through telegraph wires and print it onto paper.

welfare: help for people in need, especially money provided by government programs for problems such as sickness or unemployment.

Further Information

Books

Blumenthal, Karen. *Six Days in October: The Stock Market Crash of 1929*. Atheneum, 2002.

Burgan, Michael. *Franklin D. Roosevelt* (Profiles of the Presidents). Compass Point, 2002.

Burgan, Michael. *The Great Depression* (We the People). Compass Point, 2002.

Pietrusza, David. *The Roaring Twenties* (World History). Lucent, 1998.

Whitcraft, Melissa. *Wall Street* (Cornerstones of Freedom). Children's Press, 2003.

Web Sites

www.newdeal.feri.org Educational guide to the Great Depression from the Franklin and Eleanor Roosevelt Institute.

www.nyse.com New York Stock Exchange web site has current news, history, and information about how the stock market works.

www.sec.gov/about/whatwedo.shtml Web site of the U.S. Securities and Exchange Commission explains how the commission works and the laws that protect investors and the market.

Useful Addresses

New York Stock Exchange
11 Wall Street
New York, NY 10005
Telephone: (212) 656-3000

Index

Page numbers in *italics* indicate maps and diagrams. Page numbers in **bold** indicate other illustrations.